In his debut collection, *School for the Blind,* Daniel Simpson offers us a glimpse into the world of the blind with its attendant dangers, drop-offs, obstructions, cruelties and abandonments. Yet, here is also a world where kindnesses abound, where gestures of love by strangers and friends, alike, help to anchor the body and reconcile it to its place on earth. What is wholly surprising, as we read through the collection, is our confusion of who is blind and who is sighted. So many of the poems offer us an unusual sense of the world, a more intimate way of seeing it without the familiar visual signposts, a knowledge of it through heart and feel that the sighted can only imagine. "Most people don't realize," Simpson declares in one poem, "that I'm listening to them breathe, / that I hear body language." What a subtle and crucial way of being in tandem with others! This is what Daniel Simpson's poetry schools us to do, connecting us in invisible yet palpable ways to one another, through a second sight, a deeper measure.

— GREGORY DJANIKIAN, DIRECTOR OF THE CREATIVE WRITING PROGRAM, UNIVERSITY OF PENNSYLVANIA, AND AUTHOR OF SIX POETRY COLLECTIONS, MOST RECENTLY, *DEAR GRAVITY*

School for the Blind

Left: Dan; Right Dave

The Author with His Twin Brother, Dave, at the Age of Three

School for the Blind

Poems by

Daniel Simpson

POETS WEAR PRADA • Hoboken, New Jersey

School for the Blind

Poets Wear Prada
533 Bloomfield Street, Second Floor
Hoboken, New Jersey 07030
http://pwpbooks.blogspot.com

First North American Publication 2014
First Mass Market Paperback Edition 2014

Grateful acknowledgment is made to the following publications where some of these poems were first published or have been accepted for publication:

Atlanta Review, The Cortland Review, Disability Studies Quarterly, Margie, Prairie Schooner, Wordgathering, and *Beauty is a Verb: The New Poetry of Disability* (Cinco Puntos Press, 2011).

ISBN-13: 978-0692284575   ISBN-10: 0692284575

Library of Congress Control Number: 2014950729

Printed in the U.S.A.

Front Cover Image: Amy Monthei, "Fleeting Embers II," 2010, acrylic on canvas, 20" x 20", private collection of Dr. Ann Johannsen of Claremont Optometry Group, Claremont, CA

Photo of the Simpson twins, Dan & Dave, at the age of 3: Olan Mills

Author Photos: Karen Faulkner

Artist Photo: Amy Monthei

For my parents,
who equipped me well for this journey,
and for my brother, who has traveled this road with me.

Table of Contents

When We Were Four	3
School for the Blind	5
Kindergarten: Miss Morris	7
The Call of Poetry	8
A Blind Boy's First Glimpse of Heaven	10
Visitations of Abandonment	12
About Chester Kowalski I Don't Know Much	13
Almost Drowning	14
Mr. Gates	15
French Kiss	16
The Abduction	18
Boy Scout Friend	19
The Luxury of Being Children	20
When the Chips Were Down	22
My Excuse	24
All Day, New Friends	26
Acts of Faith	27
Vigilance and Dissembling	28
A Few Things	29
Letter to My Twin Brother	30
Acknowledgments	32
About the Author	35
About the Artist	37
About the Art	39

When We Were Four

and my twin brother and I got to jumping
on our twin mattresses,
which had lain in boredom on their wooden frames,
we put our agitators in overdrive,
turned our beds into washing machines.
Steam climbed up the wall behind our headboards.
It's hard work shaking the footboard
fast enough to spin dry a full load.
We seem to have been the first in Berwyn, Pennsylvania,
to discover you could do this.
Grampappy Armstrong just clicked his tongue.
Were we the work of the devil?
I told myself I was not afraid of the devil,
but my fear of the devil tasted like horseradish,
and my shame like the smell of sour milk.
Down the street lived a dog named Satan
who used to shit in our front yard,
and every time my Welsh grandmother said *iechyd da*
right after the grace, it would make me laugh.
Danny Boy could laugh at anything.
We were as quiet as squirrels.
We couldn't sit still at the table
because we had plastic plates and cups
and our chairs had their backs to the wall.
"Father had the shipfitter blues," we bellowed
as the sharp needle of innocence
played through the old 78 of evening
and we trampolined into the limbs of old oaks,
bouncing harder and higher each time,
hoping to stave off night and the ghost of the puppy

who had once fallen through our wild arms.
Venez, vivez avec nous, said the leaves,
promising that stars would bathe us
and the sun would dress us.
Gutten nacht, said shirts from a laundry basket,
and the bed slept, holding hands with the water pipes.

School for the Blind

Chair,
bed,
dresser.
New world
scaled down
small as the
cream-soft palms
of the four-year-old
left tonight
with his twin brother
at the boarding school
in an open dorm
(aisle nearest the lockers,
second bed down),
suitcase from home,
touch bedspread,
his hands pried
from his mother's skirt.

Best thing, she said:
braille and new playmates,
still home for the weekends.
Then they drove off.
Kathy and Connie
got to watch *Lassie*.

Down he lies.
Down he lies.

But tomorrow morning,
his shoelaces tied,

he will decide
to make new friends,
learn every language,
study the birds
to know how to sing,
read every book,
plot his escape,
and fly from the playground
on airplane swings.

Kindergarten: Miss Morris

Only later did I have the math
to figure you were around twenty-four
(college plus a year or two),
and not until ninth grade did I know
that sexual and sensual weren't the same,
though not entirely different.

I knew my hands felt rougher in the winter,
though I had no science to tell me why.
Every recess, when you held them
and rubbed them soft with lotion,
turned them over, touching every crevice,
the closest word I could find was "mama,"
somewhere in my toddler lexicon
between "mmmm" and "ah."

Some days, I bless you for this lesson
in the sensual, and for its companion,
the one in Making Change, when we played Store,
how the coins you handed me from your pocket
came with heat I didn't know I'd crave.

Now, in middle age, equipped with higher math
(two ex-wives plus multiple fractions equals
a mixed number), I am sometimes tempted
not to thank you for those early lessons
because it seems, without meaning to,
you introduced me to a Shangri-La
in the geography of my future,
then sent me off to find it without a map.

The Call of Poetry

Lickington, Waggington,
Snootsville, Barksburg:

names I made up
for the houses I passed
in my wagon, rolling down
Greentree Lane.

"Boose," a noun,
proper and common,
Dave and I made up
for simpatico dogs,

hail fellows well met
in the sleepy street
or distant criers
on backyard chains,

friendly as Jack Lemmon
singing "Howdy Friends and Neighbors,"
pattin' ya on the caboose
and shakin' your hand.

Yipper City, Velvet Ear,
Pawtucket, Tailytown.

Our own words for shoes,
toilet paper, and ears:
piggycovers, hineywipes,
waxles (from wax holes).

Chair, bed,
dresser in a dorm:
keep the rhythm running,
get from Sunday to Friday.

Lickington, Waggington,
Snootsville, Barksburg.

Miss Stout, all alone
in her first grade room,
punching out poems
while we're flying on swings.

She's putting poems into booklets
with wing-clip fasteners
so we can read their squatty lines
and call them our own.

> I sat on a broad stone
>   And sang to the birds.
> The tune was God's making
> But I made the words.[1]

Yipper City, Velvet Ear,
Pawtucket, Tailytown,
piggycovers, hineywipes,
waxles, Boose.

---

1. Second stanza of "The Day Before April," by Mary Carolyn Davies, from her second volume, *Youth Riding,* The Macmillan Company, 1919. The poem was reprinted in *Silver Pennies: A Collection of Modern Poems for Boys and Girls*, a children's reader still popular and in print today, edited by Blanche Jennings Thompson, and first published by The Macmillan Company in 1925.

A Blind Boy's First Glimpse of Heaven

I climbed the stepladder to Heaven when I was eight, my father
    spotting me from behind.
I liked that he stayed below. How else could I hear where the
    world was?

"You can move around, Son, but shuffle your feet, in case there's
    a stray
bale of hay to trip over, and you don't want to walk off the edge."

God was in a meeting, I guess. Anyway, I never saw Him.
What had He done to Lucifer? And what did the Bible mean by
    "cast him out?"

Did God have a squad of angel goons up there
to blindside Lucifer and shove him off?

I wanted to jump, to see if I'd survive.

Fifty years later, Aunt Polly said,
"You better get ready, Dan, if you want God

to take you up to be with your dad again,
and won't it be great to finally see his face?"

I don't know. I'm just getting to love
this world for what it is, a flawed place

with its subway platforms overlooking the third rail,
its hay lofts, open sewers and loading docks,

and all the strangers who've looked out for me,
letting me take their arms to walk with them.

I'm thinking, the next time I see Aunt Polly,
I'm going to tell her about my new vision:

"It's really going to be something," I'll say.
"In Heaven, you'll finally get to be blind."

Visitations of Abandonment

It came again, that same dream
trip down 95 to Florida,
all the motels full so far,
my mother asleep in the passenger seat,
my father still driving since five this morning,
me making him talk every minute or two
("How's the traffic? … Any motels lately?"),
until some question goes unanswered
(was it "Where are we now?"),
and I say, "Dad … Dad? …"

(just tires humming, that's all —
not even the radio crackling
over a fading station).
I reach up, touch
the empty seat, the orphaned steering wheel,
and though I am blind and only eight
and know nothing of driving or physics,
my bowels can calculate
mass times rate of speed.
I have never felt a road so smooth.

About Chester Kowalski I Don't Know Much

One morning, while we waited in line to see
the school nurse, he showed me how to fool a friend
through the power of suggestion.
Smacking his fist with his hand,
he pretended to crack an egg on top of my head,
then let his fingers drift like yolk down my hair.
I don't know where he learned it.
Perhaps a bigger, cooler, sighted brother,
who didn't have to go to boarding school,
duped the week before in front of girls,
had tried it out that weekend
when Chester had come home.
Or maybe it was his father who, like mine,
would show him the Full Nelson or a nest
some hornets built out back behind the shed.

I never asked him what his father did,
or what kinds of cookies his mother made for Christmas,
or his middle name,
but at night we breathed
the same fetid air of the open dorm
with thirty other eight- to ten-year-olds,
boys with healthy, shallow lungs who had played full tilt,
then said their prayers by rote —
"Now I lamey downda sleep."

I didn't know how much I didn't know
about him until they said he'd drowned
in the swimming pool. I walked past his empty bed,
heard them pack up his things,
and felt my breath against my hands.

Almost Drowning

Language left me.
Prepositions went first
when the surprised lungs
were asked to act like gills.

Adverbs and adjectives followed
as gravity toyed with me,
drawing me deeper,
letting go later each time
like an experienced seductress.

I flailed my way up for air,
for a split-second chance to sputter
out something that might save my life,
something my brother and friends might hear
in the faraway world of rope and buoy,
something to make the lifeguard remember
one Crab had moved up to Frog.

Down and down I went,
into silent darkness, without nouns,
mud sucking at my heels,
seaweed holding on,
arms heavy, so much work
left for the verbs to do —
to kick, to thrash.

Then, everything fell away,
until an "I"
seemed all there was.

Mr. Gates

When Chester Kowalski drowned, nobody said:
  Mr. Gates,
    phys. ed. instructor,
    lifeguard on duty
    — responsible.
No one said much of anything.
Gates didn't come back to school for several days,
or maybe several weeks, and when he did,
he had a different job.
Together, in seventh grade English,
we walked with Macbeth, knee-deep in blood,
sailed with the Sea-Wolf on miles of mountain-deep ocean.
We waded through book after book, and day after day,
we forgot to ask — or were dying to ask but didn't.
No one said much of anything.

French Kiss

Aunt Vivian first told me about them.
"Leave it to those French people," she laughed.
I was eleven, and suddenly I felt
something new and unnameable for her,
a wanting to be in the same room, under foot
while she baked pies, or on the wide arm
of her easy chair when she watched the evening news.

Who would guess that, a year later, I'd have my first
from a housemother at the boarding school for the blind,
an Irish washerwoman who would yell at you
if you had a hair out of place or asked for something?

That Friday afternoon my brother Dave and I
would soon be thwanking our metal white canes
down Malvern Avenue on our first solo trip
home by bus, hoping we'd find the right place
to stand and wait, not talking about what we'd do
if the driver let us off at the wrong street.

Maybe it was a sense of impending doom
that made us linger longer at her door.
Maybe it was our fledgling independence
that made us stand a half-inch taller and talk
with the ease of adults around a kitchen table.
And why was it we were suddenly learning
her husband's name, and that they both worked
in a shoe factory in Connecticut
before he died and she moved to Pennsylvania?

"Well, we'd better go," we said, sounding
like our parents' friends at midnight, when
they packed up their cards and rubbed their stiffened knees.
And then Dave walked into her room to give her a hug
(not out of the question on a good day).
I heard her stand and the crinkling of his coat,
and then silence for what seemed too long.
"Come here, Twin," she said, and so I did.
I didn't want to notice the smoker's breath,
or the false teeth that clicked when she yelled at us.
I was too surprised by gentleness to think,
too fascinated with the touch of tongue on tongue.
I'd been punished by this woman countless times.

She sat back down, and we walked to the top of the stairs.
"Have a nice weekend," we shouted over our shoulders.
We were going home with a dark secret,
and yet I felt light — in fact, so light
I slid all the way down the long banister.
How could she do anything bad to me now?

The Abduction

Maybe if I could have studied your voice
and known how to read the animal language of your animal
    body,
if I could have inferred something of your motives
as one would piece together the guitar in a cubist portrait,
then maybe I could also have had words
holy enough to summon a host of butterflies,
like emissaries from Heaven, to blind you with beauty,
or a thrush's song to stop you in awe,

and then maybe I could have said no
to the walk you proposed in the deserted clearing,
no to the beard and tongue that would swallow me,
no to the blame I thought was mine.
I could have said yes sooner to ease with others,
to life as a pantry whose shelves almost ached under the weight
    of goodness.

Boy Scout Friend

A long day of hiking, and now the man
rubs alcohol on the backs of the boy's legs,
then tucks him into the sleeping bag.
The man says good night, says he'll be back
to look in on him. The boy can't sleep;
it's those kisses on the lips.
At last he sleeps, then wakes
when the man, naked, slides in next to him.
Fingers and penis grow toward each other
like casual vines, so slow it seems accidental,
this first time to know such soft-tipped hardness
in someone, to touch this root of man,
three times his own — in age and size.
Afterward his heart pounds while the man snores.
He slowly slides out of the sleeping bag
and slips off to lie down by the dying fire.
He thinks of water — clean, fresh streams.

The Luxury of Being Children

We were lucky not to know some things as children.
Adults never said it in so many words,
but a weariness in their voices made it plain —
as though they carried boulders up a mountain
every night, while we sailed into sleep.

When Lou Quay asked Miss Walters, dorm mother
for us fifth and sixth grade boys at the School for the Blind,
to read him the Sunday paper, and she tore him apart
for being a "selfish pig," we felt we had
every right to call her "bitch" out of earshot,
or even under our breath when she walked by.
This was the Sixties, and emboldened by sit-ins and marches,
we even paid one of the special ed. guys
to knock on her door and tell her
we all said she could go fuck herself.

After a long string of days when we said, "Good morning,"
and she responded, "What's good about a morning with you?"
after yelling at us routinely to get dressed,
then standing in the dorm and chiding someone
for having no pride, being naked in front of a woman,
after berating a slew of us for masturbating,
because we'd stayed in the bathroom too long, or because
our beds had been bumped an inch out of alignment,
we were sure we had every right to tell her that.

We didn't have to wonder what made her so mean.
Why should we care whether someone had yelled at her?
What did we know, or need to know, about money,
other than how much candy a nickel could buy.
It was no concern of ours what her husband made
in the shoe factory before he died.
She never mentioned other family,
and it wasn't our place to ask her how she spent
her weekends off and whether she had friends.
Certainly, we could be forgiven
for not caring much beyond ourselves.
We all had enough to think about.

It wasn't until my senior year in high school
that my feelings for her got more complicated.
I'd left the School for the Blind, and she'd retired.
A friend called to ask if I'd heard the story:
in a cheap apartment, alone, she froze to death.

When the Chips Were Down

What else they served for lunch that day in the boys' dining room, I can't say, but, dollars to doughnuts, whatever they passed off as nutrition was anything but. It could have been their infamous sausage that greased your shirt when you first cut into it, or what they called cheese fondue, made from government surplus Velveeta and powdered eggs. Whatever it was, we'd have to count on the community bowl of potato chips at our table for eight to carry us to dinner.

Someone said grace over it because someone had to, but it was only minutes from then that the clamoring started. The housemothers stuck to their table in the far corner. Only Mr. G seemed to size up the situation.

"Satchel Page didn't have it easy, either, boys," he said. "Try to save a little for the fella sitting next to you." He leaned on my shoulder as he said this, and stretched for the empty bowl. "Let me see if the Commandant's in a giving mood." By this, he meant Miss Brennan, Head of Food Service.

She wasn't, and it didn't take long for their voices to rise above the general din and crowd it out.

"Brennan, I said these boys need more tater chips."

She said she'd put out all she was going to, and as Head of Food Service, that was her prerogative.

He repeated, "These boys need more tater chips," and when she shouted over him, he said it again, only this time like an animal that knew it could break the cage the circus had put it in.

I'd like to tell you that he stormed past her into the kitchen, that he arranged to bump her accidentally like a player might an umpire, and that he returned, suddenly calm, to set a full bowl on our table with an "eat up, boys." It's the stuff of miracles, like turning water into wine, the stuff that, on the grandest scale, makes for resurrections. This small thing being, of course, more possible, it might have actually happened. But, after all that, after all the intervening years, I don't remember. After all, it wasn't life or death. After all, it was just one replaceable man taking a losing and inconsequential stand.

By dinner, he was gone, no questions asked, including none by me. Quit or fired? I can't say. But in church the next Sunday, when the Scripture was read, I thought I heard him in the temple, shouting and knocking over tables.

My Excuse

I lit the candles, poured the wine.
You were hungry, too,
in that college room,
but for something more permanent than I.

I was still too much the young boy,
made to sleep in an open dorm,
desire and curiosity stoked
by years of being forced to play
on a cold, northern playground,
separate from the girls.

You had dreams that expanded into deep time.
All I wanted was a generous friend
in a narrow bed in a closet of a room.

Love, or so I called you then,
can you give me a free pass?

I say I only wanted
something safe and narrow,
and yet, on some blind level,
I saw the rightness of the wide and deep you hoped for —

what I hoped for,
when I sweet-talked the housemother
as I snuck a radio into the dorm.

I thought I might get lucky
and catch a wave of love song

from some station in the sun-soaked South,
a wave that would sweep me across the playground
and over its high brick wall.

All Day, New Friends

Massachusetts Youth Hostel, Summer of '99

We three rode in the back seat
of Larry's '88 Impala,
you on my left, Karen on my right, naked
except for our bathing suits and sandals,
Larry driving (it being his car) and singing
with Paul to an R.E.M. tape on tiny speakers
while we three talked about who smoked
grass, and when, and what it was like, and marijuana brownies,
and the difference between them and smoking,
our warm knees and thighs, hips and arms
rearranging themselves against one another,
as we jangled over ruts and potholes,
jangling memories and wishes loose,
so that I, knowing we were one day old together
and tomorrow this would end, said,
my breathing feeling thick, "Where were you all,
you and Karen and Paul and Larry, when
I was in high school, the first blind kid
trying to hear a few friends in the Pep Club's
Thanksgiving Eve bonfire crowd,
trying to find his way to a party
of the coolest classmates, where were you?"
which prompted Karen to say, "Yeah,
it would have been great," and you, you on my left,
to say, "Hey, what about playing basketball,
can we do that? I mean there must be a way
we can figure that out."

Acts of Faith

Friends describe colors to me:
trumpets are red they say,
clarinets purple, and oranges
taste like orange. I believe them —
no reason not to.

I buy books to read
with equipment for the blind.
It is an act of faith. In the bookstore
all the pages are blank.

At the checkout counter, I pay
with a bill that, earlier,
the grocer said was a twenty.
Or I sign a blank slip,
wherever the cashier tells me.

"No big deal," I say to myself,
walking out the door.
"Nobody knows everything."
I smell the city — oily and brown.
The yellow sun shines lemonade
which means the sky must be blue.

Vigilance and Dissembling

Since I don't see, and have no visual cues,
I'm fascinated by how sighted people dissemble.
I bet they keep their faces unflustered,
while behind their stationary eyes
another set of eyes checks you out.

I say this because, in conversation,
I try to act undivided
while, in fact, I'm on alert
for any glitch in composure,
any revelation of an actor playing a part.

It's often a matter of tone of voice.
Most people don't realize it goes even further —
that I'm listening to them breathe,
that I hear body language.
Someone talking with her right hand —
while I hold her left —
doesn't know how much I know
from the way her body moves,
as if she never touched a tie-line to a dock
and guessed the boat was bobbing up and down.

A Few Things

I don't know how they keep you on a cross
when they first start the hammering.
I don't know how they make chocolate.
I don't know which parts of a tuna they put in a can
and what they do with the rest.
I don't know what I'll do with the rest of my life.
I don't know anymore who sat
behind Bobby Sabol in fourth grade
but Allen Hawk's dad worked for the phone company.
I don't know why we tell so many sad stories.
I don't know what the skinheads next door talk about
or what the cockatiel lady likes for lunch.
I've heard that birds resolve disputes through singing contests.
I don't know what a rainbow looks like
or that my life would be better if I could see one.
I don't know why I'm writing all of this down.
I know all the vegetables in V-8 juice.
There are at least a dozen ways to say "snow" in Inuit.
I know vulnerability is related to hope
but I can't say how.
I don't know who killed the grooms in Duncan's room.
I don't know at what point you should retire a working dog.
They have three roller coasters at Knoble's Grove.
My mother belly laughed when we got splashed on The Flume.
(Or maybe it's four. I can't remember now.)
I don't know why some people give up and others don't.

Letter to My Twin Brother

I had to.
(Someone did.)
We'd outgrown our warm world,
worn out our welcome,
and so, reaching
with some vague notion
of a place to go,
I left you, breeched,
your mind still turning inward.

We make up stories
to fill the apertures in truth.
Who can blame us
for craving explanations
from time to time
to help us sleep?

Still, I'd like to think
I did not shove you backward —
I'd like to think I would have tried to tell them,
without a scrap of language,
that you were still in there.
After all, even the dumbest dog
will paw the floor and whine
to say he cannot reach a cherished bone.

The doctor smacked me,
then worked, slack-jawed and feverish,
to turn you around and bring us back together.
I waited five minutes —
forever — for you to come.

Sometimes, as you well know,
I still can plow ahead, forget to call you,
but then something slaps me up against your absence,
and I'm stopped, that newborn boy again,
listening for you.

Acknowledgments

Many thanks to the magazines where some of these poems first appeared or have been accepted for publication:

Atlanta Review:	"Acts of Faith"
The Cortland Review:	"A Few Things"
Disability Studies Quarterly:	"Vigilance and Dissembling"
Heliotrope:	"Almost Drowning"
Prairie Schooner:	"School for the Blind"
Wordgathering:	"A Blind Boy's First Glimpse of Heaven," "French Kiss," "Letter to My Twin Brother," "My Excuse," "When We Were Four"

"School for the Blind," "About Chester Kowalski I Don't Know Much," and "A Few Things" appeared in the anthology *Beauty is a Verb: The New Poetry of Disability*, edited by Jennifer Bartlett, Sheila Black, and Michael Northen, published by Cinco Puntos Press, El Paso, Texas, in 2011.

"Acts of Faith," "A Few Things," "School for the Blind," and "The Call of Poetry" can be heard on *Audio Chapbook*, a compact disc of poetry by Daniel Simpson and David Simpson, produced and released by the twins in 2007.

I wish to thank Yaddo, Ragdale, The Hambidge Center, and Wellspring House for providing oases where I could work on this book. Thanks, also, to my mentors and fellow workshop participants at Peter Murphy's Winter Poetry & Prose Getaway,

Molly Fisk's Poetry Boot Camp, and Molly Peacock's poetry workshops at the 92nd Street Y for their help in bringing these poems into the world.

Finally, heartfelt appreciation to Ona Gritz for her encouragement and invaluable feedback throughout all phases of this book.

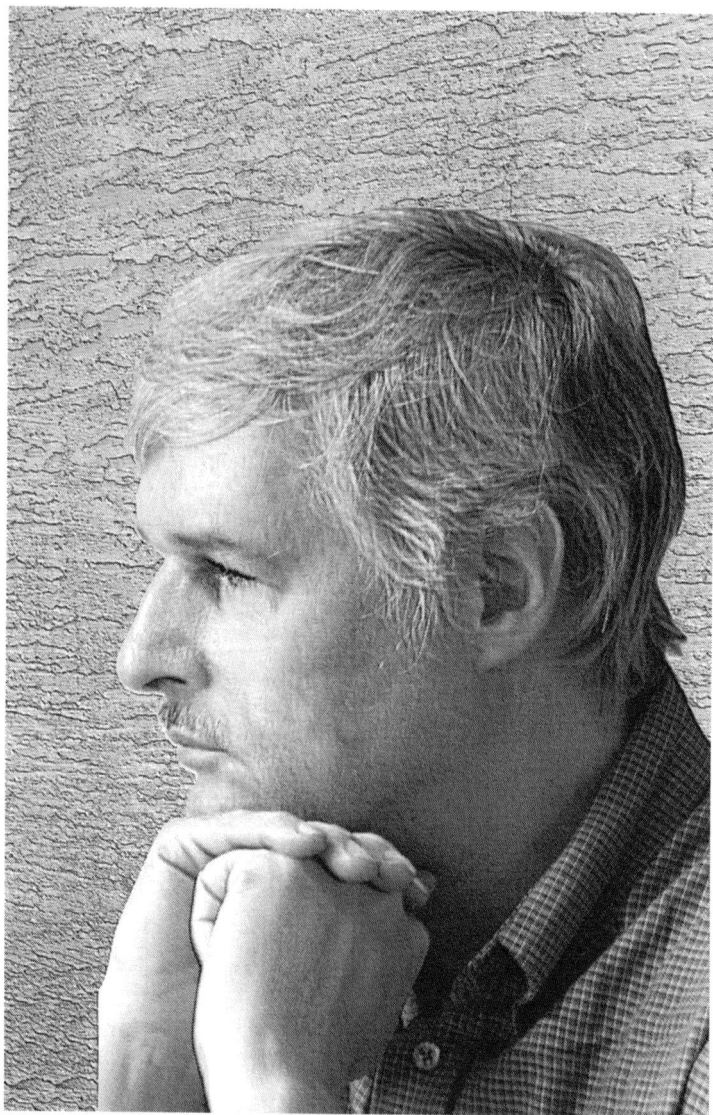

About the Author

Daniel Simpson and his identical twin brother, David, were born blind in Williamsport, Pennsylvania, in 1952. After attending the Overbrook School for the Blind through eighth grade (1956 – 1966), Dan became one of the first blind students in his county to go to a public school. He earned a Bachelor of Arts in English and music from Muhlenberg College, Allentown, Pennsylvania, where he graduated Summa cum Laude and Class Salutatorian. After receiving a Master of Music in organ performance from Westminster Choir College, Princeton, New Jersey, where he had the opportunity to sing with major symphony orchestras, Dan traveled to Paris for a year of private study with the world-renowned blind organist André Marchal. Since then, Dan has worked as a church musician, computer programmer, and high school English teacher, earning a Master of Arts in English and a teaching certificate from the University of Pennsylvania along the way.

A recipient of a Fellowship in Literature from the Pennsylvania Council on the Arts, Dan has published poems in *Prairie Schooner, The Cortland Review, Hampden-Sydney Poetry Review, Passager, Atlanta Review, The Louisville Review,* and *Margie,* among other literary journals. Cinco Puntos Press, El Paso, Texas, published his essay "Line Breaks the Way I See Them" and four of his poems in *Beauty Is A Verb: The New Poetry of Disability,* a 2012 ALA Notable Poetry Book called "unusual and powerful" by *Publisher's Weekly* in a starred review.

Dan has been invited to read his poetry at the Dodge Poetry Festival, the Free Library of Philadelphia, Philadelphia's First-Person Festival, and at the Cornelia Street Café in New York City. He's appeared at World Café Live, Philadelphia, and on WHYY-FM's *Radio Times with Marty Moss-Coane.*

Dan and his brother began playing four-hand piano and singing duets in early childhood, but their performance of popular music as a duo came into its own during high school. Even though they attended different colleges, they got together frequently to play in coffee houses during the early seventies. More recently they have enjoyed performing a show for schools, libraries, churches and conferences that combines music with poetry and tells the story of their development as artists. In 2007 the twins produced and released a CD of their poetry entitled *Audio Chapbook*.

Dan has been singing with the Mendelssohn Club of Philadelphia, a 140-voice choir, for twenty years. He serves as Access Technology Consultant to the Free Library of Philadelphia and works as a Technical Support Specialist for the Library of Congress. He and Ona Gritz are the Poetry Editors for *Referential Magazine*. His blog, *Inside the Invisible*, can be found at www.insidetheinvisible.wordpress.com.

About the Artist

I live a life filled with irony as a blind visual artist, perceiving the world from a truly unique perspective. I understand and accept these circumstances and the challenges that have assisted in shaping my own philosophy. I enjoy the exploration, not only as a personal journey but also as an art movement in itself. It is my goal, as a legally blind artist and as an advocate, to create art that is accessible, and to assist others in understanding the importance of experiencing art and the role it can play in enriching the lives of every person.

— AMY MONTHEI

Amy was born with congenital cataracts. Her lenses were removed when she was a few months old, leaving her legally blind. Her parents, who are also artists and legally blind, saw great promise in Amy's creative endeavors very early on and encouraged her with great enthusiasm. They taught her to believe that having a disability should never be perceived as being inadequate.

She graduated with Honors with a Bachelor of Fine Arts in Visual Art from Grand View University in Des Moines, Iowa. Amy worked in the fine art and custom framing industry in Minneapolis, Minnesota, for many years. Amy was also diagnosed with early onset glaucoma, and despite periods of blurry vision she still strives to create as much work as possible.

She is currently a full-time artist living in Honolulu, Hawaii, where the light and colors of the local landscape continue to inspire her creativity. Her work has been shown in many art galleries, and is included in corporate and private collections throughout the United States.

About the Art

"Fleeting Embers II" (acrylic on canvas, 20" x 20"), completed by the artist in 2010 while she lived in Minneapolis, is one in a series of paintings by Amy Monthei.

When Amy was first diagnosed with glaucoma, in 2006, she would sometimes experience days or weeks of blurry vision, creating a distortion in how she saw the world. The Embers Series was inspired by those challenging times.

The painting, along with its companion piece "Fleeting Embers I," is now in the private collection of Dr. Ann Johannsen of Claremont Optometry Group, Claremont, California.

A NOTE ON THE TYPE

This book is set in Minion Pro, an Old-Style serif typeface designed by Robert Slimbach of Adobe Systems, and released in 1990 by Linotype. Inspired by the mass-produced publications of the late Renaissance, but with a contemporary crispness and clarity not possible with the print machinery of that era, even by the best of the Renaissance typographers, this modern-day interpretation is well regarded for its classic baroque-rooted styling and its enhanced legibility. One of the five or six most widely used typefaces for trade paperback fiction published in the United States over the past several years, Minion Pro is the typeface adopted by the Smithsonian for its logo. The name Minion is derived from the traditional classification and nomenclature of typeface sizes; *minion,* the size between *brevier* and *nonpareil,* approximates a modern 7-point lettering size.